Rabaab

(Inspired by the philosophy of Guru Nanak Dev ji)

Poetry by - Seemaant Sohal

Translated from Hindi to English by - Pallavi Prasad

First Published in October 2019

ISBN: 978-93-5347-871-1

Price: INR 150/-

BLUE ROSE PUBLISHERS
www.bluerosepublishers.com
info@bluerosepublishers.com
+91 8882 898 898

Cover Design:
Mohit Joshi

Typographic Design:
Namrata Saini

Distributed by: Blue Rose, Amazon, Flipkart, Shopclues

Acknowledgment

The author hereby acknowledges the efforts made by his friends which inspired him to write this Poetry 'Rabab'.

Prologue

Perhaps some other day...

The Baba wanders
Sometimes alone
Sometimes with two disciples

Both the disciples
Follow Baba
And Baba follows Onkar[1]

Baba's thirst is great
His wanderings are greater

Some jungles
Await Baba
Some cities
Are jungles
Without him

He must make a true bargain
He must find poor Lalo's[2] house
He must teach the Kazissalat
And the Pandits - Aarti[3]
He must curse the good folks
And bless the evil ones

Baba has a lot to do

---

[1] Omkara - the syllable Om; [2] A Devotee; [3] worship by showing a lighted lamp

Only one Onkar?

One shall
Handle the self
Or one's solitude?

We too would have
Choice
Of prayers

If you oblige so, Baba!

Baba speaks
Through his disciples

Baba stops
The rolling stones

Baba sings
With the Rabab

Not a disciple
Nor a stone
Neither a Rabab
I am

Baba said a lot
I heard much less

Baba spoke through the ages
I tried to follow since then

After many stages
At last, Baba said -
"Nanak, attain such yoga[1]
That you may remain (unmoving)
In life as you do in death"*

---

[1] To unite with universal spirit; "Nanak jivteyan mar rahiyeaisa jog kamaiye"

They are very thirsty
Baba as well as
Mardana[1]

Baba a little less
And Mardana some more

Mardana remembers water
For Baba to remember (the Almighty)
Is water

---

[1] A disciple of Guru Nanak

When the Rabab plays -
Many Universes
Begin to follow
Rabab's tune

Baba's eyes fill with
Khumaar[1] and Baani[2]

Baba thinks
Mardana must wonder
Whether this music
Belongs to Nature or Rabab?

---

[1] and [2] - Hangover of divine knowledge

He roamed the jungles
He thirsted for every drop

What did you find?
If asked so
What shall Mardana reply?

In place of the father
I found Baba
So will Mardana reply

More than the mother
More than the father
More than the wife

Nanaki's[1] wait
Is greater than all

Whose vision is great
Greater is their wait

---

[1] Guru Nanak's sister

It touches Baba's Kurta
As it passes by
It dances
It sings
What does not the breeze do!

Why do I step away?
Baba's sweat
Gets irked

I wonder -
Baba's Khadaun[1] is made up
Of which branch
Of which tree
Belonging to which woods?

In which woods
Stood the tree -
Planted by whom?
Who was the doer
Of this good deed?

---

[1] Wooden sandals

Some birds
Look for Baba

In Mecca
In Medina
In Iraq
And sometimes in the land of five rivers

The birds want
To fly like Baba

The Kazi says
Allah is one
The Pandit says
God is one

Baba asks
Who is Kazi?
Who is Pandit?

Where lies the truth Baba
Hither or thither?

Truth has a great appetite
Truth is of great value
Truth takes great nurturing

If you look hither it's here
If you look thither it's there

Truth is here
Truth is there

If you wish
It is with you
If I wish
It is with me

In place of the plate the sky
In place of the lamp the sun
In place of diamonds and pearls
The moon and stars have been arranged

Baba how could you
Free the Aarti from its enclosure
Into the open space?

The Word
Minted in Sachchi Taksal[1] stepped out
And looked around

To dispense its duty
It sat upon the hot griddle
It rested upon the sword's edge
Then turned itself to the sword

The true word learned thus
How to live on

---

[1] True Mint

Broken doors
Crumbling ceiling
The courtyard is plastered with dung
Lalo's house is kuchcha

But to his home
Baba's arrival is pucca

Should I entwine around
The hands or the legs

Should I think by my mind
Or feel by my heart

Should I imbibe
Spirituality or service

Should I be Baba's
Rosary or Khadaun?

Surrounded in darkness
Bewildered
Or in dilemma
Passing through the colony of service
And the streets of love
To where this narrow path leads?

Son!
Through the Jap[1]
This path leads
To Sahib's abode

---

[1] Holy chant

In jungle
In bliss

In frustration
In satisfaction

In halting
In running

In waking
In sleeping

In singing
In playing

(One is) Sometimes Baba
Sometimes Mardana

The Hukum -
I wish to comprehend
Like sorrow
Like separation

What do you decree me
Baba?

You are permanent
You are steady
You are true
You are great
You are colorless
You are carefree
You are the beginning
You are the end

Among all that you are
Whither stands my 'I'?

I take on a good name
And roam about
Without your name*

I desire to become nameless
With your name*

---

*Hereby name the poet means reminiscing God's name

If the mind finds
Precious stones and rubies
And hunger finds mind
May the dreams find hunger

May we find
A long lappet
May we find
A thought for discipleship

We only contemplate that
May we find
What we desire

To behold innumerable sights
There are only two eyes

To hear immeasurable Naad[1]
There are only two ears

For the body
There is the only temperature

For the mind
There are only thoughts

For the heart
There is only compassion

You didn't bestow us all, Baba?

---

[1] spiritual sound or rhythm

The earth orbits the sun
The moon orbits the earth
Certainly, a body must
Orbit the moon
Whatever it be
It surely must have
A body going around it too

The Jap goes on inside them
And inside the Jap rest all

Upon skies rests the sky
Below nether lands lie the hades
The Sun is above suns
As thoughts rest upon thoughts

No Gods lie beneath the God
No Gods rest above Him

Your throne
Your beauty
Your refuge

My bed
My ugliness
My vice

The water
Belongs to Vali Kandhari[1]
While the thirst
Belongs to Mardana

Vali kandhari is alone
While
Baba stands with Mardana

Mardana's feet ache
But he does not stop

If he loses Baba
It will be hard to catch up with him

Baba looks over his shoulders
Lovingly

His look is enough to relieve
Mardana of his fatigue
And to last him a lifetime

Uncountable ragas
Uncountable musical instruments
Uncountable singers

Which instrument may play
Which Singer can sing
Your unfathomable raga?

In spite of all
Where are all?
All get left behind
Despite all

When all are there
And when they are not
You are all

The Siddha*
Jati Sati*
Indra*
Shiva*
Brahma*
All are in a trance

Beholding their trance and
Remaining steady in his own
Is the one and only AkaalPurush[1]

---

* Names of various deities;
[1] God

The blowing breeze
The flowing water
The burning fire

Deciding the properties of these three
And setting their definitions
Is the one and only AkaalPurush

Some run
Some fly
Some swim

Their goal
Igs You

Upon his kurta
May Baba wipe my tears
Some day
If only in my dream

I often think so
In my dreams

I know
You like simple food
Rather than the delicious

You like the stony path
Not the palanquin

I know
Instead of heading
To the house of the city merchant
You will come to Lalo's home

There are many eras
Many faces
Many seasons
Many lands

There is but one guise

The day my wisdom rises
That day
I shall hear the Naad

The day my wisdom rises higher
That day
I shall hear the immeasurable Naad

The day it becomes possible
That day
I will hear myself

Unison and Separation
Happened to meet once
On a path

They looked awhile at one another
And went their own ways

This too happened
After destiny's
Great device

To Bring together
To Build
To Destroy

Once again the same soil
The same idol
The same efforts

Since eternity
Exists but
One and only AkaalPurush

Crores of tongues
Crores of Simran[1]
Crores of salvations

One AkaalPurush
Keeps crores of accounts

I hold on to
Any single word
Of the Jap

There on, uncountable words
Of their own accord
Come to hold my hands

You are raw
I am ripe

It is you who is raw
Not me

You are ripe
So I am ripe

No
No

You too are raw
So am I

No
No

You are ripe.
I am raw

Baba, you may
Correct my queries
Some spellings
Some tips
Few commas
Few full-stops
As also punctuations made in uncertainty

If my questions are correct
I shall muster the courage

If I get answers to them
I shall dare ask questions

The soul swings
Without confiding in body

One tune
Is beyond all musical instruments

In trance, take place
All ragas
All plays
All spectacles

There is no definition
No logic
No curiosity even

All lie
Outside trance
Nothing lies
Inside it

I desire
To be in a unique trance
To beget unique wisdom

This being the only medium
To attain the
Wisdom of divinities

How much ever I may praise
I shall tire
Singing peans

Then, words only
Shall give me the courage
To praise more

The words that tire me
Will also be the ones
That brings me the courage
Again and again

It is difficult to be a disciple
In hardship

It is difficult to be the guru
In hardship

It is easy to be a divinity
In times of ease

Which raga is the best?
Which raga
The divinities sing best?

Raga Bhairavi
Raga Malkauns
Raga Kaharwa

Or the raga of Trance?

A face peeks from behind the screen
Wearing a long robe
Sat Kartar[1], Sat Kartar - he calls

Just as you raise
The screen to look
The Baba who does not beg
Moves on

Chant His name
Work hard
Share and eat
Thus he says

---

[1] God is truth

Where no one may seek accounts
No one may comment
Where I will not be cheated

What is devotion
What is salvation
Who is God -
Where no one may tell me

Upon the earth
Upon another planet
Or within me
There is a place (for Him)

Not in devotion
Nor in trance

I am in Khumaari[1]

---

[1] Hangover

Tiny droplets
Of water
That seems like shower

Will drench
Your hearts and minds

Such words as these
Will certainly have been
Minted at the Sachchitaksal

Huzur

What is near
What is far

What is salt
What is motichoor[1]

Who is fakir
Who is houri

When you'll reach the Darbar*

The milk will part
With water

---

[1] An Indian sweetmeat;
* meaning the God's court

As long one does Simran
So long lasts the toil

As long one does Simran
So long lasts the fragrance

As long one dies Simran
So long lasts the dilemma

These are other names for Simran -
Toil
Fragrance
Dilemma

A song rings
Through the trance
Into the soul

The trance snaps
In an effort
To catch the tune

Then
That very trance
Helps to regain the tune

On a rainbow swing
I swing in fear

Mixing the color of Simran
I create an eight colored swing
That is stronger
Greater
More beautiful

Then I swing on
Fulfilled

Small hands
Small thoughts
Small prayer

Big praise
Big throne
Big Sahib

Few
I pull a little tight
Few
I leave a little loose

Few strings be tuned high
Few be low and uncertain

Hence a new music
Will be created
For a new trance

Thus my Rabab
Will be retuned

A bundle of thoughts
A bundle of silences
A bundle of illusions
A bundle of egos

A bundle of heads
That loads all these bundles

If it gains the sense
To know His command

All bundles will become light
And easy

The Shiva sings
Brahma sings
Mahesh sings

The sun scorches and sings
The wind sings in whispers
The water sings in gurgles

All sing
Hence I sing

I open to see
Each word

To find a sitar
An Iktara or
A Rabab therein

Like holy note
Found in musical instrument

Gild few worries
In some courage

Give away paths
To few jungles

Curse some folks
Of few villages

Even this will
Make the world more habitable

Do oblige, Baba!

I take off my shoes
Before going up the Holy stairs

I bow my head

I listen to Gurbaani

I return to again
Put on the shoes of my ego

What you feel right
Is right

What you do not feel right
Is not right

I repeat all this
At every step
At every breath
Birth after birth

What month
What season
What was the time when

The universe was created
The universe was improvised
The universe was contemplated

What prevailed in the mind
Of Akaalpurush then?

My power
Is not mine

My knowledge
Is not mine

My thought
Is not mine

So why be forceful
And against whom?

The hukum
Be His

Who gives
Refuge

Who knows
Between a few words
Between a few lines
Few boats may be seen asail

Who knows
Which boat may suit you and
Make you float in the river of emotions

My brother
My friend
My child
When you study
Focus
When you listen
Focus
Upon the Japuji*

A book of chants written by Guru Nanak

Leaves
Flowers
Trunk
Then as I sing
I reach the roots

Then the soil
And the moisture

Assuming
That even a tree
Must possess a soul

Beyond the windows and doors
Far into yonder
In some corner of the sky
A hawk cuckoo sings
As it flies

A dark and dense
Cloud of Gurbaani
Breaks rain
On hearing the bird's song

A dense jungle
Speaks to the trees
Reveals to the birds

The Baba
With his two disciples has
Traversed the villages
And the jungles
It remains for him to rest under the trees
And hear the birds sing

May it not happen
That I will be left out
May it not happen
That you get left behind

Pray thus
Thus pray

A thorn
Wants to touch
Baba's feet
And weep upon them

But Baba knows
Before it can prick,
The thorn
Shall break into tears

Mardana asks
Baba reveals

Mardana plays music
Baba sings

Mardana runs
Baba holds him

The thirst
Seeks knowledge
The hunger
Understands it

The summer is bewildered
And the winter is in a dilemma

The villages scratch their head
And the jungles stomp their feet

The winds murmur
And the waters eavesdrop

Baba
Smiles to himself

The AkaalPurush
Must look after love
Love needs to do nothing
Than be there

May there be Khumaar
I wish to lose all in it
In Khumaar
I want to break the rut and reach you
In Khumaar I want to understand my state

One day in Khumaar
May I reach from 'I' to 'you'.

When I pray
May I be honored
When I pray
May I gain strength
When I pray
May I be content

What should I do
To gain this sense to pray?

When did he stumble on questions
When did he not find answers

How many times
He beheld thirst
How many times
He understood thirst

When did he want to run away
When did he want to stop

Upon Mardana's escape
And his awakening
Throw some light, Baba?

The sky
The hades
The sun
The moon
The earth
Are all devotees of God

They are in rhythm
They are bound to Him

If you say life
Life it be
If you say death
Death it be

Every time
Again and again

You will repeat thus
So I shall too
Repeat this

Baba is
Preceded by silence

He is succeeded
By an era

Beside him
Is Mardana

When Baba asks a question -
Mardana looks for something
He sees something
He follows something
And thus he wonders

The nature of words
Must be changing
When you say
"Baani[1] has come from the fount
Dissipating all worries"*

A word itself
Must tell you
I am not for this season
Do choose my synonym?

---

[1] Divine knowledge or preaching;
* "Dhurkibaaniayi tin saglichintmitayi"

As one walks in the scorching heat
There must be blisters on one's feet

Mardana must be happy
To find an excuse to camp

Baba must be pleased
To see Mardana happy

At Baba's touch
The blisters must have taken a new meaning

Due to God's
Insistence
I reminisce him

Then halfheartedly
In reminiscence
I persist

Although
I know
That God knows this

I am bent
Beneath my sorrows

Had I bent
With humility
It would be another thing

Had it been so
It would have been worship

Beholding the sun -
Revolving between seasons
Holding hands with the moon
Providing food to creatures
Of innumerable identities
And keeping nothing in memory

Why does the earth not think about all this?
I casually ponder

Many colors
Many forms
Many guises

Many Krishna
Many Shiva
Many Brahma

Many suns
Many moons
Many earths

Many winds
Many fires
Many waters

Many preachings
Many meditations
Many austerities
Many salvations

The AkaalPurush
Is but one

In the Gyaankhand*
One may rest, one may proceed
Again rest, again proceed

Hastening on
Is barred on this premise

---

*Premise of knowledge

The rustling of Kurta
The clatter of Khadaun
The chatter of Mardana

One must do Jap
One must be austere
One must give oneself

Not ahead
Nor after
But alongside Baba

Truth is slow, lie is quick
Truth lags, lie leads

The wait for the truth
Lasts long
The pleasure of lie
Lasts long

The bigger lie is that
One can win upon the truth
Easily
The bigger truth is that
The lie will not forego one's trail
Easily

The Gods were created
The demons were created

Just when Trust missed its creation
Hope was created

One scathing sun
And a cool sip

One scorching sun
And a small sap

One heavy downpour
And a soft palm

Are nature's bane
As well as boons

In the state of trance
There is no thought
And among endless thoughts
There is no trance

If trances were attained
Thoughts would cease

Life and death
High and low
Well and unwell

- That we take birth and we die
We rise and we fall
We do well and we subside

As per his command

I saw Baba
I saw him drown
I drowned in the sight of Baba drowning

Thereupon
I saw nothing

Some tricky questions
Posed to father Kalu
Some disturbing questions
Made to mother Tripta
Some chaste questions
Put to sister Nanaki
Some profound questions
Asked to wife Sulakhni

He who himself is the answer
To every Paandha*
What to ask Baba?

Pleadings and prayers
If they are within praises

I shall plead more
And pray more

I shall devote
Myself less

How many universes
These many universes
As many universes

Baba beholds through
The telescope of Jap

I pass through
food-grains and water
Reach the plate
Look at the hands
Contemplate upon the tongue
Enter the stomach -
I Turn to bones and marrow

I eat to my fill
Thanking the AkaalPurush

Every word
Every line
Every page
Their meanings puzzle me

Surely this path
Must lead to the land of knowledge

I understand
So I may speak

Lest I gain the sense
To know this

It is my questions that
Stop me from actions

I too want to listen
I too want to sing
I too want to have fun

Lest I find
The answers to a few questions